Rooftop Astronomer

Rooftop Astronomer

A Story about Maria Mitchell

by Stephanie
Sammartino McPherson
illustrations by Hetty Mitchell

A Carolrhoda Creative Minds Book

Carolrhoda Books, Inc./Minneapolis

For my parents, Marion and Angelo Sammartino, who told me girls could do anything

Since Maria Mitchell's time, we have learned that it is *never* safe to look directly at the sun, not even through sunglasses or smoked glass. Radiation from the sun can pass through even darkened glass and damage the eyes.

Library of Congress Cataloging-in-Publication Data

McPherson, Stephanie Sammartino.
    Rooftop astronomer : a story about Maria Mitchell / by Stephanie Sammartino McPherson ; illustrations by Hetty Mitchell.
        p.   cm. — (A Carolrhoda creative minds book)
    Includes bibliographical references
    Summary: Recounts the life and accomplishments of the first woman astronomer in America.
    ISBN 0-87614-410-5 (lib. bdg.)
    1. Mitchell, Maria, 1818-1889—Juvenile literature. 2. Women astronomers—United States—Biography—Juvenile literature.
    [1. Mitchell, Maria, 1818-1889. 2. Astronomers.] I. Mitchell, Hetty, ill. II. Title. III. Series.
    QB36.M7M36 1990
    520'.92—dc20
    [B]   89-28885
    [92]   CIP
                                                                  AC

Manufactured in the United States of America

1 2 3 4 5 6 7 8 9 10 99 98 97 96 95 94 93 92 91 90

Table of Contents

Introduction

The large hall in Philadelphia was jammed with people. It was 1876, one hundred years since the United States of America had declared its freedom from England. But American women were still fighting for equal rights with men. The president of the American Association for the Advancement of Women took her place at the speaker's platform.

Maria (pronounced ma-RY-ah) Mitchell surveyed the large crowd and waited to begin her speech. Although the people before her were a blur of unfamiliar faces, she herself was well known to everyone in the audience. Maria had become famous almost thirty years earlier when she had discovered a comet from the rooftop of her parents' home.

The discovery of a comet was not a rare event in the nineteenth century, but women astronomers were very rare indeed. Maria was the first woman astronomer in the United States, and she was determined not to be the last. That's why she spoke at women's rights meetings and taught astronomy at Vassar Female College. She felt it was important to encourage young women to be anything they wanted to be. In her early years, Maria had had someone to encourage her too.

Not many girls who were born in the early 1800s were lucky enough to have a father like William Mitchell. A dedicated astronomer and teacher himself, he was delighted with the early talent his daughter demonstrated for science. Instead of considering such an interest useless for a girl, Maria's father did everything he could to further her knowledge of mathematics and astronomy. Maria's diligence and the outstanding contributions she made to science, education, and women's rights more than repaid her father's enthusiastic efforts.

1

Nantucket Childhood

Maria Mitchell's black, curly hair blew in the wind. Her arms and legs were covered with goose bumps beneath her plain Quaker dress. It was cold on the rooftop of her Nantucket home at night, but it was also exciting. Gazing down at the nearby wharf, Maria could see dozens of ships. Most of them were whaling vessels. Their tall, straight masts, ghostly in the moonlight, seemed to point straight to the stars.

"Maria!" called her father softly. Still peering through the small brass telescope, he beckoned eagerly. Maria pressed her eye to the telescope, careful not to move the instrument. She immediately forgot all about the chill in the air and the whaling ships in the harbor.

But whaling was the main reason Nantucketers, young and old, studied the stars. Most families on the remote island off the coast of Massachusetts counted at least one whaler among their members. Whalers and other sailors studied the stars to learn how to navigate their ships through vast, empty stretches of ocean. Friends and relatives of whalers also studied the stars. It was one way to feel closer to their loved ones far at sea.

Most of the houses in the town of Nantucket, as well as some houses in the outlying areas of Nantucket Island, were built with a platform on the roof called a widow's walk. Widow's walks were named for the women who would climb up to the rooftops and look far out to sea to watch for the safe return of their husbands' ships. The platforms also provided an unobstructed view of the stars.

Maria would have liked to spend all of her time studying astronomy, but she also had to study other subjects. Maria had already learned to read by the time she started school in 1822, when she was four. But there was a big difference between reading at the kitchen table with her mother and going to an unfamiliar school with a teacher she didn't like at all. Although Maria liked her second teacher better, her favorite teacher would always be her father.

Mr. Mitchell had such strong feelings about the way children should be taught that he decided to open a school of his own. During the early nineteenth century, book learning was not considered important for girls. Mr. Mitchell disagreed. He taught both the boys and the girls in his class to think for themselves, to explore nature, and to ask lots of questions. And Maria, who was one of his students, *never* ran out of questions.

The equality in Mr. Mitchell's classroom was partly a matter of his Quaker religion. Quakers believed that girls deserved the same quality of education as boys. Maria's father was also influenced by the spirit of Nantucket itself. Nantucket women enjoyed an unusual amount of freedom. Because their husbands might be at sea for several years at a time, the women had to be able to take care of themselves and make their own decisions. No one questioned their right to participate fully in the life of the island. They spoke their minds freely on school, town, and church matters, and they were listened to with respect.

Certainly Mr. Mitchell's own sense of justice and his relaxed personality contributed to the opportunities for all of the students in his class. Maria's father was much more tolerant than many of his fellow Quakers. He loved bright colors and music, two pleasures strongly discouraged by his religion. The gardens about the Mitchell house overflowed with flowers, and there were pink roses blooming on the wallpaper in the sitting room.

Other colorful objects brightened Maria's home. A glass ball suspended from the ceiling of the sitting room acted as a prism and set blue, green, red, and yellow rainbows dancing in the corners. Mr. Mitchell's collection of minerals sparkled red and blue and purple in the sunshine. And there were planets in the attic. The "planets" were wooden balls, up to a foot in diameter, that Maria's father had painted bright colors. He had used them in a model of the solar system.

Maria was in the sitting room one afternoon when, to her astonishment, the wooden solar system came tumbling down the two flights of stairs from the attic. It was First Day—the Quaker Sabbath—a time set aside for quiet reflection.

Maria had been doing her best to concentrate on her First Day reading, but the sudden invasion of the noisy spheres set her giggling at once. There went the sun and the moon. Saturn was wobbling crazily toward the fireplace, while the asteroids crashed into table legs and chairs.

Maria's younger brother and sister pounded into the room after their runaway playthings. Although Maria knew that it was not proper to play games on the Sabbath, it wasn't long before she joined the frantic chase.

Maria would never be too old for a good laugh or a childish romp. She preferred lively conversation to the heavy silence of the Sabbath. Instead of sitting quietly in her Sabbath clothes, she would rather be digging on the beach, playing with her brothers and sisters, or—best of all—focusing the telescope on a faraway star. Fortunately, studying the stars was one of the pleasures that was not forbidden on First Day. When darkness fell, no matter the day, Maria and her father were certain to be found on the roof.

One winter day in 1831, however, Mr. Mitchell stationed the telescope in the window of the front parlor. It was a cold day, but the glass had been removed from the window. Usually Maria avoided the stuffy, formal parlor. But today the twelve-year-old astronomer had a job to do. Sitting at a table near the telescope, she bent over a chronometer, or ship's clock. Her father watched proudly as she counted the seconds before the beginning of the coming eclipse. Soon the moon would pass directly between the earth and the sun. For a time, it would block out most of the sun's rays, and day would turn to twilight.

Maria's brothers and sisters crowded around the table. Andrew, Sally, Ann, William Forster, Francis, and Phebe did not share their sister's passion for astronomy, but they did know that an eclipse was an important event. Baby twins Henry and Eliza were too young to know what was happening.

In spite of the crowd, Maria concentrated intently on her task. At exactly 11:55 and 7 seconds, she recorded the beginning of the eclipse in her notebook. It wasn't dark yet, but that would soon be changing.

Peering through a piece of smoked glass to protect her eyes from the sun's rays, Maria watched the eclipse. Never would she forget the excitement of seeing the moon march across the face of the sun. Years later she still spoke of her wonder at seeing a sunny day turn dark hours before its time. Even the animals outdoors seemed confused, and some of the chickens went to roost for the night.

The moon advanced until it appeared to cover the sun completely. Then slowly it passed beyond the sun, and daylight returned to the streets of Nantucket.

Sometimes, Maria knew, scientists traveled hundreds of miles to study an eclipse from a favorable position. She often wished she could travel too. When Maria grew restless, she would roam the island's beaches and rolling countryside. She collected stones, seashells, and seaweed on her many ramblings. At the Sankaty Head cliffs, she sometimes found small fossils. Fossils always delighted Maria—they were full of mystery, just like the stars. Maria called them "autographs of time."

If Maria ever got lost on one of her walks, all she had to do was wait for nightfall. She could guide her course by the stars as surely as a sailor.

Maria soon discovered something she could do even better than a sailor. It happened the day Captain Bill Chadwick entered the little gray house on Vestal Street, where the Mitchells lived.

Captain Chadwick didn't bother to knock. He simply lifted the latch, a strong wooden one salvaged from a wrecked ship, and strode into the hallway. On Nantucket, visitors often entered without knocking, so Maria's mother was not surprised. She was regretful, however, when she noticed the chronometer he was carrying. Mr. Mitchell was away from home, she explained. He would not be back in time to correct the chronometer for the captain's next voyage.

Maria watched the disappointed captain with the precious instrument in his hands. So many times, she had helped her father with this kind of work. Couldn't she do it by herself? All at once she was sure she could.

But Maria's offer to help was met by silence. Captain Chadwick needed the chronometer to help him steer by the stars. The safety of his ship and crew depended on its accuracy. Maria knew this and met his questioning look with a confident gaze. In the end, Captain Chadwick decided to trust her with the job.

All the rest of the day, Maria thought about her task. She knew she could do it, but she couldn't help feeling a bit apprehensive. She could hardly wait for nightfall so she could get started.

When the stars came out, Maria was ready. Using her father's instruments, she carefully measured the positions of various stars. She noted the exact time of each observation on the chronometer. Maria used her calculations to correct the instrument so it would keep accurate time at sea. Captain Chadwick was delighted when he saw the chronometer, for Mr. Mitchell himself could not have done a better job.

Time to Start Work

"Maria, Maria! Tell us a story!" All day long, Maria's brothers and sisters kept after her. They never tired of listening to her tales.

But sometimes Maria wished she had more time for her books. At sixteen she was already a teaching assistant to a schoolmaster, and she continued to study on her own. She was not thinking of a professional career; she continued her studies because of a sense of wonder at the beauty and intricacy of the universe. There was so much to learn and so little time to study.

In desperation Maria tacked a sign to the door of her tiny study beneath the attic stairs. "Maria Mitchell is busy. Do not knock." But no sign could stop the children from demanding Maria's services as a storyteller. And no studies, however important, could keep Maria from giving in to them. With a sigh and a smile, she would launch into a tale.

One of the children's favorite stories was an old Indian legend about a giant sachem, or chief. Walking along the beach one day, the sachem got so much sand in his shoes that he pulled them off and threw them into the sea. One of the sand-filled shoes became the island of Martha's Vineyard. The children loved to hear how the other shoe became their very own island of Nantucket.

Now that Maria was old enough to have a job, she was also old enough to worry about money. Acting on a friend's unsound advice, Mr. Mitchell had lost a great deal of money, and the family was having trouble making ends meet.

Maria knew the money she earned was important to her family, but she was unhappy with the rigid atmosphere and strict discipline of the school where she worked. So, when she was seventeen, Maria decided to open her own school. She found a large room in a building on Trader's Lane where her class could meet. Then she put an ad in the newspaper, inviting all girls age six or older to attend.

The day her school opened, Maria sat nervously facing the rows of plain wooden benches. As the students drifted in, some of them were nervous too. Not all the girls could afford the tuition.

Most of the schools for older children on Nantucket were called cent schools and charged only a penny a day. Maria had to charge three times that much. But some children had only a penny to offer Maria. Maria set them all at ease when she quietly accepted their money.

A small black girl hesitated at the back of the room. She was not allowed to attend Nantucket's free school, she explained in a soft voice. Could she come to this new school? Maria smiled broadly and beckoned her into the room. She lost no time in making the girl feel welcome. It didn't matter to Maria that others might not like her policy. All children—black or white, rich or poor—would find a willing teacher in Maria Mitchell.

Maria put the older girls to work helping to teach the younger ones. There was always a lot of noise and activity in the big room, but no one seemed to mind—least of all, Maria.

In many ways, Maria's school was different from any other school on the mainland or on Nantucket. Sometimes she and her students met before dawn or after sunset. They watched how animals behave in the early morning hours. They learned about stars and planets and seashells and rocks. In a way, the whole world was Maria's classroom.

Even so, the school closed after one year for lack of money. Maria wanted more than ever to help support her family, but there weren't many opportunities for an eighteen-year-old girl in 1836.

Then Maria had a wonderful piece of luck. She was asked to be the librarian of Nantucket's Atheneum Library. It was the perfect job for someone who loved books. Maria would earn a good salary, she would have plenty of time to study, and her evenings would be free for her to continue her astronomical observations. Maria could hardly wait to begin her new duties.

Still more good fortune was in store for Maria's family. Mr. Mitchell got a new job as cashier of the Pacific Bank on Main Street. Not only was the pay good, but the fancy living quarters attached to the bank would be available for his use.

It wasn't easy for Maria to say good-bye to the little house on Vestal Street. At first she felt lost in the large, grand rooms of her new home. But she liked the big kitchen in the cellar, and she liked watching the whalers and merchants bustle about their business on Main Street. And Maria was delighted to have her very own room at last.

Best of all was the observatory on the roof, with its brand-new equipment, including an expensive four-inch telescope. The telescope was on loan to help Mr. Mitchell do star observations for the United States Coast Survey. As his assistant, Maria would take measurements that would help sailors use the stars to determine their ship's exact position at sea.

Maria made some new friends through her work for the Coast Survey. One of these was Professor William Bond, who was in charge of the observatory at Harvard University. Maria became especially close to the professor's son George. Since George was also an astronomer, he and Maria had much to talk about. Whenever she could, Maria would take the half-day steamer ride to the mainland to see George. On one of these visits, she and George became, with the professor's help, two of the first people to see the newly discovered planet of Neptune. George's visits to Nantucket were less exciting astronomically—he came more to see Maria than the stars.

During her many visits to Harvard, Maria came to greatly respect Professor Bond's skills as an astronomer. She thought he must be a genius. Maria knew that she was not a genius. "I was born of only ordinary capacity, but of extraordinary persistency," she once said.

And night after night, Maria persisted in her observations from the roof of the Pacific Bank. If the sky was clear, not even the coldest weather could stop her. As Maria's log books accumulated through the years, so did her knowledge of the stars.

But one hot July night in 1846, a dense blanket of smoke blotted out the stars over the island of Nantucket. A fire had broken out in a hat shop and was roaring down Main Street. The blaze was approaching the Methodist church near the Pacific Bank. Some men thought the church should be blown up before the fire reached it. Without that large wooden structure to feed it, the fire would be easier to fight. The bank and other important buildings might be saved.

The men dragged barrels of gunpowder through the smoky streets to the church. But before the gunpowder could be ignited, Maria Mitchell appeared out of the crowd. She loved the beautiful, old building and could not bear to see it destroyed while there was the slightest chance it might be saved. Maria ran up the steps of the church and turned toward the men. Her face was dirty, and her hair was disheveled. She could feel the heat of the fire as it drew nearer and nearer.

Fiercely she dared the men to blow up the church. For a tense moment, Maria and the men stood facing each other. Then, before anything was decided, the wind changed. The fire veered in another direction, and the church was saved.

Not pausing to rest, Maria rushed through the hazy streets back to the bank. Some sparks had landed on the rooftop observatory. By the time she arrived, many valuable records had been destroyed and some of the instruments had been damaged. Soon there was more bad news. The Atheneum Library had burned to the ground. None of the books had been saved.

When the sun rose the next morning, the Nantucketers were shocked to see how much of their town was in ruins. But the islanders were tough and used to hard work. They lost no time in clearing up the rubble and setting out to replace what was lost.

Maria helped rebuild the observatory over the bank. Proudly she watched new buildings go up on the sites of the old ones. A new library, an exact duplicate of the old one, was built, and its shelves were lined with new books. Within six months, Maria was once again a librarian by day and an astronomer by night.

Maria Mitchell's Comet

It was a clear autumn night in 1847, and Mr. and Mrs. Mitchell were having a party. One minute Maria was there mingling with the guests, and the next minute she was gone. Those who knew her well did not wonder where she had disappeared to. At age twenty-nine, Maria loved watching the stars as much as she had when she was twelve. No party, no matter how lively, could keep her from the rooftop observatory.

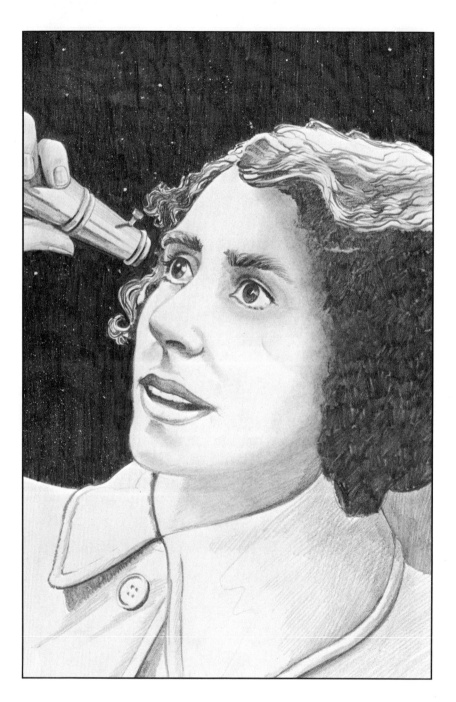

Quickly Maria threw a cloak over her shoulders and grabbed a lantern. Then up through the attic she climbed to the roof. As she focused the telescope, Maria forgot all about the gathering below.

Suddenly Maria stiffened. She stared, first in puzzlement, then in mounting excitement. All she saw was a tiny, blurry light like a very faint star. But Maria knew the sky well enough to be sure there had been no star in that position earlier. What was this strange new light about five degrees above the North Star?

Only one explanation occurred to Maria, and it was so thrilling, she hardly dared to think about it. Her heart beat rapidly as she clattered down through the attic again.

Back at the party, Maria whispered in her father's ear. At once Mr. Mitchell rose to follow her to the roof. Soon he too was gazing at the faint, fuzzy light.

Maria could not see the light at all without the aid of the telescope. She waited anxiously for her father to finish with the instrument. Finally Mr. Mitchell turned back to his daughter. He believed she had discovered a comet.

Maria and her father recorded the comet's

coordinates—a set of measurements used to indicate a position in space—so other astronomers could find it. But when Mr. Mitchell wanted to write Professor Bond about the discovery, Maria protested. What if they were mistaken? It would be better to watch the comet for several nights more, she argued. If it moved during that time, they could be certain of their finding.

The next day, a wild storm blew across Nantucket, but by evening, the sky had cleared a little. Maria was able to find the light and see that it had shifted position in relation to the stars. It *was* a comet! But no ships could leave the island with the mail that day or the next because the weather was still too violent. Mr. Mitchell's letter, dated October 3, 1847, finally left for the mainland on October fourth.

When Professor Bond received the letter, he used Maria's calculations to locate the light. It was definitely a comet, but was Maria the first person to discover it? Might someone else have seen it first? This was a very important question because the king of Denmark was offering a gold medal to the first person to find a "telescopic comet," which was a comet that could only be seen through a telescope.

Professor Bond and George were very excited about Maria's discovery. They observed the comet for several nights. Then on October 20, Professor Bond wrote to Denmark to claim the gold medal for Maria. The prize, however, was not so easily won. One man in Rome had seen the comet just two days after Maria. A man in England had found it one week later.

It was too bad there had been so many delays. The contest rules stated that the discovery of a new comet must be reported immediately. But Maria's champions did not rest. Edward Everett, president of Harvard University, wrote many letters for her. So did the Bonds.

One year and many arguments later, the winner was announced. Maria Mitchell had won the gold medal. With trembling fingers, Maria opened the small box that came in the mail one day. Carefully she studied the gleaming medallion. It said, "Non Frustra Signorum Obitus Speculamur et Ortus." Maria knew Latin well enough to read the inscription. "Not in vain do we watch the setting and rising of the stars," she translated. These words described Maria's feelings perfectly. All of her life, she had watched the stars, and for the rest of her life, she planned to keep doing it.

A Whole New Life

Maria's life was never quite the same after she won the medal. She still worked at the library. She still climbed to the roof at night and made observations for the Coast Survey. But now Maria was famous. It bewildered and amused her.

Newspapers all over the country told the story of Maria Mitchell's comet. Scientists she'd never met wrote letters to congratulate her. Tourists visited the library just to catch a glimpse of the woman astronomer. What they saw was a strong-featured, almost stern-looking woman with dark eyes and a mass of black curls. Her direct gaze and blunt manner added to her forbidding appearance.

But if the visitors watched the librarian with her friends, the young people who came to seek her advice, they saw a very different Maria Mitchell. Then Maria's eyes softened, and a warm smile lit her face. She loved chatting with her young friends and broadening their world through books.

A whole new world was opening up to Maria too. The American Academy of Arts and Sciences voted her its first woman member. So did the Association for the Advancement of Science.

Maria was asked to work on a nautical almanac, a book with information about the tides, the phases of the moon, eclipses, and the movements of the planets. She joined a staff that included many famous scientists. It was a great honor, but it was also hard work that would have to be repeated year after year. Sometimes the mathematical calculations seemed endless. Assigned the tables of Venus, Maria worked a year or more in advance to determine the positions that planet would occupy in the sky.

Maria was soon traveling more often too. She attended scientific meetings in New York and visited her friend Joseph Henry, director of the newly founded Smithsonian Institution, in Washington, D.C.

During her travels, Maria began to realize how independent Nantucket women were. It amazed and angered her when she saw what little respect women seemed to command on the mainland. Champions of women's rights were ridiculed for their views. Very few young women were encouraged to think for themselves or to take an interest in science or mathematics. And even on Nantucket, women were not allowed to vote. Maria hoped that someday all this would change.

By this time, the older Mitchell children had married and left home. Maria was in her thirties, long past the age when most women married. For a while, it seemed that Maria's friendship with George Bond might ripen into a deeper relationship, but it never did. Perhaps Maria felt that she had to choose between marriage and a career. Perhaps she felt she was too old for George, who was seven years her junior. Whatever her reasons, Maria was content to remain George's friend. They continued to correspond even after George married someone else.

Maria kept herself busy and happy, but sometimes she felt isolated on her faraway island. She enjoyed visiting Washington, D.C., and New York, but she wanted to see the rest of the world.

Maria's chance came in 1856 when she received a letter from a rich man named General Swift. He wanted her to accompany his daughter Prudence on a trip to the southern United States and to Europe. Although the general had never met Maria, he had read all about her and thought she would be the perfect traveling companion for his daughter.

Maria longed to take the trip. But how could she leave her almanac work and her mother, who had not been well for some time? Maria's family insisted that this was an opportunity she must not miss. She could take her almanac work with her, her sisters argued. They would see to it that their mother was well cared for in Maria's absence.

Within a few weeks, Maria was sailing down the Mississippi River to New Orleans. Not long afterward, she found herself aboard an oceangoing vessel at last. Maria was on her way to England.

England for Maria meant carriage rides through the narrow streets of London, trips to great-domed observatories, and meetings with famous scientists to whom she carried letters of introduction. At the Greenwich Observatory, overlooking the Thames River, she stood at the point of zero longitude, a thrill for someone who had spent many hours figuring distances from that very point.

But Maria's adventure had barely begun when word came that General Swift had lost all his money. Prudence had to return home immediately, and Maria had to decide whether or not to accompany her.

Although her funds would be limited, Maria decided to remain in Europe. There were still so many scientists to meet and places to see. She moved from her elegant lodgings to a small attic room and worked diligently on her almanac calculations for a month. Then she bravely set off for France on her own.

In Paris Maria started on another round of sightseeing and visiting famous scientists. She roamed the marketplace, visited churches, and attended lectures. She soaked up the colorful sights and sounds of the city.

But the place Maria was most eager to see was Rome. When she heard that her friend Nathaniel Hawthorne and his family were setting out for the ancient city, she decided the time had come for her to leave Paris too. Maria had been introduced to Mr. Hawthorne, who was a famous American writer, in England. When she asked if she could join his family, he was happy to agree.

Maria and her new friends made their way across the picturesque countryside of France and Italy by coach. They stopped at primitive inns where hard bread and goat cheese were all the owners had to offer. In Italy they had to travel a lonely road known as a favorite haunt of bandits. Maria hid what little money she had in her stocking. As the coach approached Rome, night began to fall. Occasionally Maria caught a moonlit glimpse of men carrying long guns. What a relief it was to arrive safely in Rome.

Maria had hoped to see the famous Vatican Observatory while she was in Rome, but she was disappointed to learn that women were not allowed inside. It took several weeks for Maria to get special permission to visit the observatory. Even then she was not allowed to stay after dark and view the stars through the Vatican telescope.

It was a memorable experience just to visit the observatory by day. Maria thought of the great astronomer Galileo, one of the first people to realize that the planets revolve around the sun. Not far from where she stood in the observatory, Galileo had been forced to deny his beliefs because people still wanted to believe that the earth was the center of the universe. Maria thought about how horrible it would be to deny a scientific truth.

Although it had been a wonderful trip, Maria was not sorry when the time came to go home. She missed her family and was especially worried about her mother.

When Maria's ship docked in Nantucket, only her father was waiting for her. He tried to prepare her for the changes in her mother. The illness had affected her mind, he explained sadly. Moments later, when Maria rushed to embrace her mother, Lydia Mitchell did not recognize her. How Maria wished she had left Europe in time to be properly greeted by her mother.

Work was all that could take Maria's mind off her mother's illness. Soon she had settled back into her busy routine. While she was in Europe, a group of women had collected money to buy Maria a new telescope. They wanted to honor the first woman astronomer in the United States. They also wanted to give her an instrument that would help her do her finest work.

Anxious to live up to the faith placed in her, Maria set to work in her new observatory behind the schoolhouse. She studied sunspots and double stars, she wrote papers about astronomical events, and she looked for comets.

In 1861 Maria's mother died. Although Maria had always loved Nantucket, she and her father decided to move to Lynn, Massachusetts, on the mainland.

As the only unmarried daughter, Maria felt an obligation to care for her father. She would keep him company and make sure the household ran smoothly. But one of her first jobs would be to set up her telescope. No matter what else changed in her life, Maria would always have her work.

Women in a
Changing World

One day a letter arrived that surprised and delighted Maria. She was forty-four years old and her curls were turning gray, but suddenly she was as excited as a young girl. Maria was being considered for a teaching position at Vassar, one of the first women's colleges in the United States.

Maria had read newspaper articles about Matthew Vassar, the wealthy man who had donated the money to found the college. Vassar believed women deserved the same opportunities that men enjoyed. He wanted women to have the finest education available in the country.

Many people thought Mr. Vassar's ideas were ridiculous, and some newspapers made fun of the school. Editorials claimed that women were not strong enough for serious study. They said that women would become thin and pale and sickly if they went to college and would never become good wives and mothers.

Maria shook her head when she read such statements. Long hours and hard work had never weakened her. She might have been amused if she hadn't been so angry. What were women supposed to do? she wondered bitterly. If a woman had the keen eyesight and nimble fingers for delicate embroidery, then she could just as easily focus a telescope or note fine distinctions in the colors of the stars.

Maria longed to be part of Mr. Vassar's new college so she could share her enthusiasm and inspire future scientists. But she worried about her own lack of a college education. Was she really qualified for the position? The school wasn't even in Massachusetts. It was being built in Poughkeepsie, New York. Was it fair to up-root her father again so soon after the death of her mother?

For a time, Maria's doubts were put aside. The Civil War broke out, and all building on the college had to be postponed.

After the war, Maria had another obstacle to face. Some of the people in charge of the new college did not like the idea of a woman professor. Maria was indignant. How could it truly be a college for women without any women professors?

Although Mr. Vassar agreed with Maria, he had to fight to get his way. But the founder's wishes were realized at last. Persuaded by her father, her friends, and her own wishes, Maria accepted a position with the college.

On September 21, 1865, Maria stood at the front of her empty classroom. She felt a little like the seventeen-year-old girl who had opened her own school on Nantucket. The young women entered the classroom and sat down. They were very quiet as they waited for Maria to begin. They were also very quiet when the class was over. Maria wasn't sure what to make of so much silence.

Finally a student in the first row spoke. The young woman admitted that she had always considered science dull. Her first astronomy class, she hastened to add, had been anything but dull.

Maria broke into a smile. She was going to succeed after all.

Maria's students were not always so quiet. Late one evening, a cry of excitement rang through the freezing air. It was followed by another, then a third and a fourth. The students in the dormitories couldn't sleep for the noise, but Maria's students continued to shriek with delight every time a new meteor flashed across the sky.

It was twenty degrees below zero. The young women shivered under layers of cloaks and scarves. Their fingers and toes felt like ice. Still they stayed to count the meteors as they fell. When hundreds and thousands of meteors fall in a single night, it is no time to think of the cold.

From time to time that night, Maria took her students down to her living quarters for some hot coffee and a place by the fire. Conveniently, her rooms were located right in the observatory itself. But scarcely were her students warmed up when it was back to the meteor shower again.

Of course, there was nothing in the college rules about students staying up all night to watch meteors. The rules stated clearly that all lights must be out in the dormitories by ten o'clock. But that didn't stop Maria. Down the halls she would run at any hour, summoning her students to see an unexpected meteor shower or, in rarer instances, a comet. There was nothing the dormitory supervisors could do to stop her.

But astronomy wasn't all midnight excitement. Being an astronomer also meant making careful observations, recording findings accurately, and learning to measure precisely. Many of the mathematical calculations that had to be made were very difficult. Maria's dedication to and faith in her students made the hard work worthwhile to them. They loved their kind, outspoken, and demanding professor. The students were also fond of Maria's father, who shared her quarters at the college. Mr. Mitchell remained an avid astronomer until he died in 1869.

Unfortunately Maria wasn't always as popular with the college officials as she was with her students. She made no secret of her dislike for grades, and she never marked attendance. These things were not important to Maria. Her students were learning. They came to her class because they wanted to know more about the universe. That was all that mattered to her. But the college officials thought grades and attendance were very important.

Maria had another strong opinion that dismayed some of the officials. She wanted women professors to receive the same salary as men. More and more women were being hired by the college. Why should the women do the same work as the men for less money? When nothing changed despite their protests, Maria and another woman decided to take drastic measures. They would quit their jobs.

Because of this threat, the women were given a small raise in salary. Even though she still earned less money than the male professors, Maria felt that a partial victory had been won. She decided to stay at the college.

Maria did everything she could to help women gain power in education and in other fields. In 1873 she went to New York for the first meeting of the Women's Congress. Many of the great women of the time attended the meeting, including Elizabeth Blackwell, the first woman doctor in the United States; Antoinette Brown Blackwell, the country's first woman minister; and Julia Ward Howe, the famous writer. Also present were the well-known champions of women's rights Lucy Stone, Elizabeth Cady Stanton, and Susan B. Anthony. Like these other famous participants, Maria Mitchell believed that women should have the right to vote and to own property. They should be free to express their political and social views in public.

Although Maria enthusiastically supported the goals of the new organization, she was surprised to be elected its president for the third annual meeting. The third session of the Women's Congress was held in Syracuse, New York, in 1875.

No one who saw Maria standing straight and tall on the speaker's platform could have guessed how frightened she was. But Maria knew her message was too important to let her personal feelings stand in the way of her delivery.

Maria waited until the crowd in the hall had quieted, then she spoke of the purpose of the new organization. She said women should be encouraged to enter all professions and to involve themselves in government. She called for a survey to discover how many women felt stifled in narrow, boring lives and how many were reaching for broader horizons. She said that, most important of all, the new organization should help all women to recognize their unique gifts and to use them for the betterment of their country and all humankind.

Maria spoke with so much common sense and feeling that her audience was deeply moved. Many people—men and women—went home from the congress with entirely new ideas about women's roles in society.

Lifetime Added
to Lifetime

It was one thing to be nervous before a large group, but it wasn't like Maria to be shy about approaching a friend. "Have you a bit of land behind your house in Denver where I could put up a small telescope?" she finally asked her visitor at Vassar.

"Six hundred miles," came the swift reply.

Overwhelmed, Maria thanked her friend warmly. No longer would she worry about a place from which to observe the coming solar eclipse. As the moon passed between the earth and the sun, the moon's round shadow would fall upon the land. Denver would lie within the area of that 116-mile shadow. This meant that people in and around the city would experience a total, rather than a partial, eclipse.

Maria was almost sixty years old in July of 1877

when she set off by train for the West. One of her students came with her. Another student joined Maria in Cincinnati, and a third student boarded the train in Kansas City. Two more were waiting to greet her in Denver.

Then the anxiety began. The trunks containing the telescope lenses did not arrive. For two days, Maria and her students haunted the railroad station. When their luggage finally did appear, the rain began. It poured for three days. The day before the eclipse, hail fell with the rain.

Impatiently Maria waited for the weather to improve. A cloudy sky would blot out the eclipse entirely, making the whole trip a waste of time.

The next day dawned fair and clear. With great relief, Maria and her five students pitched their tents on a hill overlooking a high plain. In the distance loomed the snowcapped Rocky Mountains.

Maria assigned one of the girls to the chronometer to count the seconds before the eclipse began. It was always hard to determine the precise instant when the moon seemed to touch the sun, but it was important to know. Accurate time-keeping would provide valuable information about the moon's movements.

Maria and her students donned dark glasses to protect their eyes. As the time for the eclipse drew near, the little group fell silent with anticipation.

When the moon had almost covered the sun, a bright halo surrounded the moon's black disk. This was the sun's corona, which appeared to fling glowing streamers far into space. It was only visible for a short time, but just a glimpse of the incredible spectacle made the entire journey worthwhile.

Maria always taught astronomy by sharing her work with her students. They helped her in the observatory. They watched her take photographs of sunspots. They studied the rings of Saturn and discussed Maria's ideas about what they were made of. They listened to her theories about Jupiter and watched its satellites travel across the face of the planet.

Absorbing as all this was, Maria stressed that the workings of the universe were not easily uncovered. "It is lifetime added to lifetime that leads to the discovery of law," she said.

This was one reason teaching was so important to Maria. She knew there was only so much she could do, but her students would carry on after her. In turn, they would train a new generation of scientists, male and female, to carry on after them. Maria worked hard to instill her painstaking methods and her attention to detail in each of her students.

But once a year, Maria's students got to put aside their books and have some fun. Once a year, the great observatory was transformed by tables and candles and roses into an elegant banquet hall. The students talked and laughed as they spread sun-shaped balls of butter on rolls that looked like crescent moons. Maria's dome party was the highlight of their year, and Maria loved it just as much as her students did.

Maria even wrote poetry for these festive occasions. Since each student received a short verse about herself, Maria sometimes spent weeks preparing her "dome poetry." Once she told her students, "I have written you each a poem, and I have told you that you are all angels." Surely there was a twinkle in her eyes when she added, "We shall see whether you are so foolish as to believe it."

At one party, Maria's students decided to play turnabout. Climbing onto the steps that led to the great telescope in the dome, they arranged themselves into a chorus and began to sing. The tune was the familiar "Battle Hymn of the Republic," but the words were all their own.

> We are singing for the glory of Maria Mitchell's
> name,
> She lives at Vassar College and you all do
> know the same,
> She once did spy a comet and she thus was
> known to fame,
> Good woman that she was!

Maria smiled as verse after verse was sung. When she discovered the comet, she could not have known that one day a group of young women, her own students, would be singing about it. Maria's unexpected fame had led to many wonderful opportunities. Now she was helping create a world where hard work and dedication were enough in themselves to open doors for women.

For many years, Maria continued her work at Vassar. She held her last dome party in June of 1887 and shortly afterward, became ill. Bouts of dizziness and memory lapses forced her to retire the next year. Maria died in 1889 in Lynn, Massachusetts, but her students remembered her for the rest of their lives.

Not long after Maria's death, some friends and admirers founded the Maria Mitchell Association on Nantucket for the continuation of her astronomical observations and other scientific studies. Maria Mitchell had earned her place as an inspiring educator, a champion of women's rights, and a tireless and ever-questioning scientist.

Afterword

In 1986 another young woman discovered a comet. Working at Mount Palomar Observatory near San Diego, California, Christine Wilson had equipment and techniques at her disposal undreamed of in Maria's time. At the start of her career, she had a knowledge of astronomy surpassing all that Maria learned in a lifetime of study.

But Christine Wilson's discovery, while exciting and well publicized, did not catapult her into sudden fame as Maria's had. New comets are not headline news. Thanks to pioneers like Maria, neither are women astronomers. Women now occupy important positions in the scientific community. Side by side with their male colleagues, they fight disease, predict the weather, design computers, and continue to discover comets. Maria Mitchell would be pleased.

Sources

"Maria Mitchell Memorabilia" (72 scrapbooks on microfilm). Courtesy of the Maria Mitchell Association, Nantucket, Massachusetts.

Books:

Kendall, Phebe Mitchell. *Maria Mitchell, Life, Letters, and Journals.* Boston: Lee and Shepard Publishers, 1896.

Morgan, Helen L. *Maria Mitchell, First Lady of American Astronomy.* Philadelphia, Pennsylvania: The Westminster Press, 1977.

Wilkie, Katherine. "Maria Mitchell, Stargazer." In *Women Who Dared to Be Different,* edited by Bennett Wayne. Champaign, Illinois: Garrad Publishing Company, 1973.

Wright, Helen. "Maria Mitchell." In *Notable American Women, 1607-1950, A Biographical Dictionary,* edited by Edward T. James, vol. 2. Boston: The Belknap Press of Harvard University Press, 1971.

Wright, Helen. *Sweeper in the Sky: The Life of Maria Mitchell, First Woman Astronomer in America.* New York: The Macmillan Company, 1949.

Pamphlets:
(Courtesy of the Library of Congress)

Albertson, Alice Owen. "Maria Mitchell, 1818-1889." Reprint by permission of *Vassar Quarterly,* February 1932.

Babbitt, Mary King. "Maria Mitchell as Her Students Knew Her." Copyright 1912.

Mitchell, Maria. "Address of the President." From "Papers Read at the Third Congress of Women." Chicago Historical Society, 1875.

Mitchell, Maria. "The Collegiate Education of Girls." From "Papers Read before the Association for the Advancement of Women," 1880.

Mitchell, Maria. "Recent Astronomical Phenomena." From "Papers Read before the Association for the Advancement of Women," 1884.

Whitney, Mary W. "Life and Work of Maria Mitchell, L.L.D." From "Papers Read before the Association for the Advancement of Women," 1891.

The author wishes to thank Dr. Jane Stroup and Kitty Pochman, librarians at the Maria Mitchell Association, Nantucket, Massachusetts, for their assistance in the preparation of this book.